ENDING AMERICA'S POLITICAL PARTIES

BEFORE THE PARTIES CAN END AMERICA

A brief history and opinion piece

by

uTAH jAY©

DEDICATION

This is dedicated to you, the American people.

ACKNOWLEDGEMENTS

I wish to thank my friends and editors Heather Anderson, Jared Anderson, and Dayle Sant for their time and efforts in bringing this brief history and opinion piece to its fruition.

~ Jay Sant (uTAH jAY ©)

ENDING AMERICA'S POLITICAL PARTIES

BEFORE THE PARTIES CAN END AMERICA

A brief history and opinion piece

Today we Americans, having grown into a great society, have come to find ourselves smack-dab in the middle of a grand and marvelous state where everything good and evil seems to be moving at the speed of sight into one fantastical plaything after another – computers with Cortana™ or some other intelligent personal assistant and knowledge navigator to research anything, smart phones that do what we ask like turning on and off our lights at home when we are several states away, beds that automatically adjust to our size, weight, sleep preferences, and even programmable cars that drive themselves – so we no longer have to think for ourselves but instead can play more games, watch more movies, more porn, more TV shows on every portable device imaginable, anywhere we happen to be at any given time, text incessantly and anonymously with few repercussions, and have all our earthly needs met with very little effort on our part. Between this abundance of idle time and the busy hours spent trying to earn a living, few people in America today make the effort to see or care about what is going on in our Federal Government other than that which can be caught in a few quick glances of this evening's fabricated television news cast or on some pod-cast put together by some angry soul who couldn't even begin to name the Three Branches of Government. But in Government there remains the age old question that has haunted mankind since the days of Adam: Is mankind capable of ruling himself or must mankind be ruled over? Must man be ruled by some king, like King George III who reigned over an entire empire with an iron fist, an empire which stretched the width of the globe and included her new colonies of America, Canada, India, and Australia?[1] Or must mankind be dominated by some tyrant, like Hitler who murdered millions out of religious jealousy[2] or by monsters like Stalin,[3] Mao,[4] Castro,[5] or Kim Jong-un of North Korea who murdered hundreds of millions of innocent people just to show those who remained alive that they had best stay in line knowing that their new government could kill and would kill at the slightest provocation? Or must we be ruled over by some zealot from today's divided streets, you know, the strong man who leads the most vicious mob to victory at the local place of higher learning and then decides that all of those who are different from him and his must be eliminated if they won't become blind followers?

Now this age old question of who will rule is further complicated by use of the "plaything" in the first sentence that has distracted way too many Americans from the real problems at hand in these very troubled days, one of which is the problem of who will rule whom. The sad truth is that way too often the simplest solution seems to be the answer for far too many of today's citizens. Consider the automatons we see with their heads bent down and their necks kinked at every possible moment while their eyes are glued to their Smart device as they walk unknowingly into the goldfish pond at the local mall or the good folks at Sunday service who seem more interested in their Smart devices than they are in what is being said at the very service they got up early to go to. Just imagine what this does to their children who are watching their every move as well as other people's children who are watching them as they become the "shining example" of what one should do when the intended message becomes the least bit boring. Are they not afraid that their bodies will get stuck in that staring and scrolling position forever just as their mothers warned them that

---

[1] https://en.wikipedia.org/wiki/George_III_of_the_United_Kingdom

[2] http://www.telegraph.co.uk/news/1481975/The-Holocaust-death-toll.html

[3] https://historyofrussia.org/stalin-killed-how-many-people/

[4] http://www.independent.co.uk/arts-entertainment/books/news/maos-great-leap-forward-killed-45-million-in-four-years-2081630.html

[5] http://www.conservapedia.com/Fidel_Castro

their eyes and mouth would become stuck when making faces at the dinner table? But ask the man with the Apple™ in his hand to give a quick synopsis of the 4th or 5th Amendment to the Constitution and watch as his eyes glaze over waiting for another chance to take a peek at that plastic wonder box waiting in the palm of his hand, just waiting there all nice and warm, begging to be looked into again. But I digress…

At the time of the founding of America, after England and good old King George had made us a slave holding colony in order to satisfy their insatiable desire for cotton and other raw materials, man had not ruled himself since the very dusty days of the Anglo-Saxons. Then America fought and won a war with England, the wealthiest and most powerful nation on earth, a nation that possessed the most dominant army and navy on earth. This great war was fought because the people of America, a new and backward colony in King George's mind, had been taxed unjustly and without representation, and they were ruled over by this very king, the tyrannical King George III who never so much as ventured across the waves of the Atlantic to see just who or what it was he was ruling over, a despot who would have his way no matter the cost to man, God, country, or tea. This is when the Founding Fathers of this Great and soon to be Free nation asked themselves once again, that age old question, Is man capable of ruling man -- of ruling himself -- or must man forever be under the control of some king, tyrant, or worse yet a murderous dictator like the 20th century's Kim or Mao?

***

To be ignorant of what occurred before you were born is to remain always a child.
~ Marcus Tullius Cicero

To answer this question, the Founding Fathers searched history. They searched the Bible, particularly the five books of Moses. They studied the great societies like Israel, Greece and Rome. They read Cicero. They studied the Anglo-Saxons, the great Anglo brothers Hengist and Horsa who brought to the shores of England, around 450 AD, the idea of "peoples law" a law so basic that it did not need to be written down, as it had become common knowledge that a thief, a murderer, or anyone who does harm to another must be punished. They searched high and low for any form of government to study, and they studied them all sincerely. From their studies, the American Founding Fathers brought forth on this earth, by the admonition and the assistance of God, a great society based on the idea that men are created equal by a loving and caring Father in Heaven. And because of this they finally knew that not only was man able to rule himself, man was *meant* to rule himself because all men are created equal (regardless of what falsehoods some modern historians try to force down our throats) and that no man, not even King George III, could be born higher or lower than any other man, healthy, wealthy, or not.[6]

This was a new order for the ages as is stated on the Great Seal of the United States of America, "Novus Ordo Seclorum" which is Latin for A New Order for the Ages. The Founders accomplished this with the creation of three documents, the Declaration of Independence, the Constitution of the United States of America, and the Bill of Rights, documents that would forever change the course of not only America but all of mankind. These documents would at long last bring hope through the ages, the hope of freedom to uncounted billions around the world. They would finally lift up all who were willing to dream, lift them up and out of the oppression of kings, socialists, or even worse, communists. Meaning, if people were willing to study hard and to work even harder toward their

---

[6] *The 5000 Year Leap*, W. Cleon Skousen, (copyright 1981, National Center for Constitutional Studies, April 2009 edition), pp. 12, 15-18, 37-47.

desires, they could at long last actually achieve the very pinnacle of their desires, while those who lived before these documents had no right to their dreams, no right to their ideas, and no right to their creations. These three documents brought forth into the world the realization that with much study and hard work, individuals – any one of God's children, from no matter what station in life, from any color, creed, or sexual persuasion – could lift himself or herself to the very height of power, fame, and wealth. What these documents meant for the first time in the written history of mankind was that not only the Heads of State – the monarchs, their children, family, and friends – but all of mankind, from the lowliest of birth to the highest of the mighty could at long last behold and achieve the greatness that our Father in Heaven has built within each of His children. And, yes, that means you and me and your neighbors, too, including the ones who do not go to church or are members of another religion or those who are simply avid fanatics of Comic-Con. Everyone.

Now this was the conclusion reached by the Founders of America, the idea that made these United States the greatest nation among all the nations of earth, the unique idea to leave the citizens of this great nation free to pursue their own lives without the interference of government, no more and no less.

* * *

Freedom is not a gift bestowed upon us by other men, but a right that belongs to us by the laws of God and nature. ~ Benjamin Franklin

If this is your dream -- to be the owner of your work, your ideas, your inventions, your art, your words -- if this is something you wish to see brought back to your children, to your neighbors' children, to all the children of God -- then we are all, for all intents and purposes, going to have to be missionaries. Our ***mission*** is to bring to fulfillment once again the dreams of the Founders of this now Politically failing nation with its new monarchy of the Political Parties, and to bring these dreams back to our families, our friends, our neighbors, and to all who will listen to these words of truth, the words that have been lost in the bitter battles of the Political Parties and those who would seek to divide the American people for their own rewards, *and we must do this with all civility.* We must remember that we are God's children and that it was God's plan for the American colonists to divide themselves from the tyranny of Mother England, to throw off the yolk of British colonial rule, therefore, it must be God's plan for the children of all mankind -- for all men are created equal -- to divide themselves from any form of tyranny that holds mankind down.

But *first*, we must separate ourselves from the lies and the contention of the Political Parties, whose only purpose, in conjunction with the American media, seems to be to divide the people of this great nation by pitting one Party against another. Our nation has always best thrived when united, but today's Political Parties have divided the American people for their own Political purposes and their own power, their own needs and their own riches of gold and silver. Recently the public electorate voted the Republican Party into the office of President, rejecting the Democrat Party that had held that office for eight years. But has anything really changed? Bitter bickering between the Parties and even within the Parties remains. Very little has been accomplished to improve the lives of the American people.

And too often those we have elected to Federal Political Offices do not have to abide by some of the laws which they impose upon the rest of us. An example is the Affordable Care Act which, although mandatory for the general public, is not required for these Politicians during the time they are in office or even after. Another example is their legal freedom to indulge in insider trading in the Stock Market, where the rest of us would be imprisoned for the same action. Are they really so elite, so far above us, that they consider themselves American demi-gods? We must remember, and remind the elected officials, that they are our employees. They work for us, not we for them.

* * *

I think one of the first things we Americans need to know is what kind of a government we live in, a Democracy or a Republic? I can tell you right off the get go here that we Americans do not live in a Democracy, even though almost every politician, news reporter and commentator, and teacher you have ever had tries to tell you as much, as often as possible that we do live in a Democracy. I can tell you why we do not have a Democracy very simply. You see in a Democracy the majority always wins and there is no recourse for the losers. In other words, a Democracy is like two wolves and one sheep voting over what's for dinner, and when the votes are counted the sheep has no rights, no recourse to protest the outcome of the vote. In a Republic, on the other hand, the sheep has a sheep dog to protect the sheep's rights, and a vote, as do all the other sheep.

As a matter of fact, we pledge to our Republic form of government every time we say the Pledge of Allegiance.[7]

Pledge of Allegiance.

I pledge allegiance to the flag
Of the United States of America,
And to the <u>REPUBLIC</u>
For which it stands,
One nation, under God, Indivisible,
With liberty and justice for all.

---

[7] http://www.ushistory.org/documents/pledge.htm_Emphasis on Republic added

7

The Constitution of the United States of America formed a **REPUBLIC** not a Democracy. In a Republican form of Government, we elect people who represent us -- who supposedly think as we think -- for different terms of governmental office like President, Senator, Representative. A Democracy is an entirely different form of government that gives the popular vote supreme legislative power. It is a form of government that no more respects the rights of its citizens than it recognizes the Good Lord who gives the people these rights which we find in our founding documents.

In a Democracy, the people meet and exercise the government in person; in a Republic they assemble and administer it by their representatives and agents. A Democracy, consequently, must be confined to a small area. A Republic may be extended over a large region (Federalist papers, No. 14, Page 100.)[8]. Democracies have ever been spectacles of turbulence and contention, have ever been found incompatible with personal security or the rights to personal property, and have in general been as short in their lives as they have been violent in their deaths (Federalist papers No. 10, page 81)[9].

After reading these references and many more, and knowing how intently the Founders of this great Republic studied to find just the right type of government they needed for a free people, I am positive that they did not choose a Democracy. As a matter of fact, after the Continental Congress had met and made their decision on the form of government, Benjamin Franklin was asked by a citizen what sort of government the delegates had created. His answer was: "A Republic, if you can keep it."[10]

As you might be able to see today, our Republic is getting very

---

[8] https://www.congress.gov/resources/display/content/The+Federalist+Papers#TheFederalistPapers-14
[9] https://www.congress.gov/resources/display/content/The+Federalist+Papers#TheFederalistPapers-10
[10] **Richard R. Beeman, Ph.D. as found on** https://constitutioncenter.org/learn/educational-resources/historical-documents/perspectives-on-the-constitution-a-republic-if-you-can-keep-it

difficult to keep with so many who do not know our history or have been misled as to the truth of our history. So why is it that so many of our leaders, including teachers, professors, politicians and news commentators (especially Tucker Carlson of Fox News Channel fame who really should know better) tell us that we live in a Democracy when anyone with a small knowledge of American history knows we are a Republic? The answer to that is complicated and has been influenced by several factions over the last century, factions working to undermine our free Republic. This is a discussion for another day. Suffice it to say, if we think about the words we utter as we recite the Pledge, we realize that it is a Republic and not a democracy to which we pledge our allegiance.

****

"When the representative body have lost the confidence of their constituents, when they have notoriously made sale of their most valuable rights, when they have assumed to themselves powers which the people never put into their hands, then indeed their continuing in office becomes dangerous to the State, and calls for an exercise of the power of dissolution." ~ Thomas Jefferson

As I think of my many years of being an American citizen, I simply cannot remember a time, any time, except perhaps a short while during the Reagan administration, when we Americans have been brought together and unified by our Political Parties for any reason, not even in times of war when the lives of American children have been laid on the line by these very Political Parties. Nor have the Parties ever worked together for the unmitigated good of the American people, for it is the very objective of Political Parties to defeat one another whenever and wherever possible and by whatever means possible and almost always with the help of the American news media, a media which of necessity feeds on bad news and feasts on ugliness. "Why worry so much about truth" the media seem to think, "when there are sheep to be eaten?!" The media faction of today has taken the opportunity of political division between the Parties to enrich itself by reporting lies and half-truths while letting the people fend for themselves as to what is and what is not the truth. This is bringing the people of this great country to a boiling point of political division that may well lead to a new civil war, a war such as has not been seen in this great country of ours for more than one hundred and fifty years. But why should the media care when there is so much money to be made?! So much gold and silver!

This must stop! The division of the people by the Political Parties must be brought to a quick and bloodless end. The American media must be made to pay a very high price for their outright deceitfulness and treachery as they erroneously inform the American people, crimes of the highest degree that must be paid for by the majority refusing to listen to and support them. Now, in our day, just as the American Founders threw off the yoke of British colonial rule and just as President Abraham Lincoln and freedom loving Americans defeated the Confederacy and freed the slaves, we dedicated Americans must begin the task of throwing off our partisan masters the Political Parties and their partners in the media and on Washington D.C.'s K Street, home of the so called think tanks, advocacy groups, and lobbyists. Once again, we must free the people of this nation from tyranny and disunity, the results of lies, innuendos, and half-truths of the Political Parties and their media partners.

These Political Parties, most especially Republican and Democrat, are the very instruments that are, now more than ever before, dividing the American people with their feigned bitterness, their falsehoods, and their outright lies. The Political Parties, the Progressive Republicans and the Progressive Democrats along with the media's fake authenticity, do not unite but rather divide us so they can enrich themselves as never before with power, fame, gold, and silver.

George Washington warned us against forming Political Parties and of their deceitfulness and greed. It was in his farewell address that George Washington publicly warned the American people of the ill advised use of Political Parties. He believed that these political factions would one day seek to obstruct the execution of the laws that had been created by the rightful government and that these Political Parties would try to prevent the branches of this rightful government, designed to keep one another in check and remain balanced, from enacting the very powers provided to them by the Constitution. He warned that such factions may well claim to be trying to answer the popular demands of the people or simply trying to solve a problem for the people but that the Parties' true intent would be to take power *from* the people of this great Republic and place it within the hands of unjust men and women, i.e. Politicians. President Washington recognized that it is natural for people to organize into groups such as Political Parties, but he also recognized the tendency of these Political Parties to seek more and more power for themselves and to take revenge on their political opponents which weakens the very government they profess to stand for. They would distract the governmental servants of the people from their true and rightful duties. They would create unfounded jealousies among different groups and regions solely for their benefit. They would raise false alarms among the people. They would promote riots and unrest. They would form other unjust groups to benefit them, fight for them, disrupt the public for them, and make a show for their lap dogs, the media. And one day the Parties may well provide foreign nations access to the very government they profess to be working for and are sworn to protect.[11]

---

[11] *The Real George Washington,* Jay A. Parry, Andrew M. Allison, W. Cleon Skousen, (copyright 1991, 2008, National

Does it sound to you like George Washington is right here with us in these days of our trying times?

****

It was Alexander Hamilton, one of the authors of *The Federalist Papers* and first Secretary of the Treasury, who said, "I never expect to see a perfect work from an imperfect man."[12]

What he meant by that was that this nation did not need or want its leaders to be polished men and women in ten thousand dollar suits and twelve thousand dollar designer dresses, to flaunt power and position as many first ladies have, showing off their luxurious living thanks to the people's expense while their husbands, in many people's opinion, were running our country into the ground. For example, when a very recent President came to office he and his family had barely a million dollars to their name, but when they left just 8 years later their net worth was $12.2 million,[13] quite a trick, me thinks, with an annual Presidential salary of $400,000 and a mere $50,000 non-taxable expense account.[14] This was by no means an isolated case.

In the days of the Founders, good men were expected to leave their families, their occupations, or their farms to come to the houses of government for a term or maybe two with the true intent of making our country a better place in which to work, play, worship and create, and then return to what they had come from and let other good men go and do the same, **instead of making themselves richer and more powerful, like the men and women who currently populate Washington, DC**. The last thing the Founding Fathers envisioned for this country is what we see

---

Center for Constitutional Studies, sixth printing 2009), Also visit nccs.net

[12] http://www.great-quotes.com/quotes/author/Alexander/Hamilton/pg/3

[13] https://www.bing.com/search?q=barak+obama++net+worth&qs=SC&pq=barak+obama+&sk=SC6AS1&sc=8-12cvid=5EDC1371A9374E36995FCACDF8E6F919&FORM=QBRE&sp=8

[14] https://www.sapling.com/7800283/presidents-yearly-salary

today, a government populated by those who base their "service" to the people of this country solely on what power, privilege, and riches they can muster for themselves and their families, like the John McCain's, Lindsey Graham's, Orin Hatch's, Maxine Watters', Chuck Schumer's, and the Nancy Pelosi's. In addition, there are many others in both Houses of Congress and those whom they appoint to lifelong positions in the different branches of government who do their own bidding and their Party's bidding instead of working for the betterment of all the American people. They are a prime example of the power and privilege we now see openly displayed inside the beltway that is today's Washington DC. The Founders never wanted their dream to be worked by those of wealth, power, or fame alone. The Founders sought to make such things as power, privilege, fame, and fortune irrelevant to those who serve in government. Although this was not meant to bar those of power and privilege from serving in government, it was surely meant to exclude those who wished to acquire such fame, power, and fortune for themselves and their families simply by *pretending* to serve the people. The Founders thought the service alone to be the privilege. In a speech given to the Continental Congress, Washington accepted the commission to be Commander in Chief of the Continental Army but requested that he not receive a salary for his service, only that his expenses be paid at the conclusion of the war.[15]

***

One of the ideas that developed in this great Republic was that of American exceptionalism. This came about in a time when America made most of the world's products, fed most of the world's people, and saved the world from fascism as a result of World War II. Americans rebuilt Europe

---

[15] https://www.loc.gov/rr/program/bib/ourdocs/commission.html, Primary Documents in American History, George Washington's Commission as Commander in Chief

and protected our allies from Communist threats. We were actually called the Bread Basket of the World then...sometimes we still are. Now I know that as of late we have had an American President who actually said that he believed in American exceptionalism as an Englishman might believe in English exceptionalism,[16] but to me this was trite and disdainful coming from a man who accused the United States of America of being a Colonialist nation imposing our will upon the countries we helped. It is the United States of America that the world calls on when troubles come to their shores. We give more, make more, feed more, and help more people in need in this world than any other nation.[17] This concept of helping in the world without colonizing the conquered is best described by the following words of General Colin Powell, former Secretary of State:

"Far from being the Great Satan, I would say that we are the Great Protector. We have sent men and women from the armed forces of the United States to other parts of the world throughout the past century to put down oppression. We defeated Fascism. We defeated Communism. We saved Europe in World War I and World War II. We were willing to do it, glad to do it. We went to Korea. We went to Vietnam. All in the interest of preserving the rights of people.

And when all those conflicts were over, what did we do? Did we stay and conquer? Did we say, 'Okay, we defeated Germany. Now Germany belongs to us? We defeated Japan, so Japan belongs to us'? No. What did we do? We built them up. We gave them democratic systems which they have embraced totally to their soul. And did we ask for any land? No, the only land we ever asked for was enough land to bury our dead. And that is the kind of nation we are."[18]

---

[16] http://www.factcheck.org/2015/02/obama-and-american-exceptionalism/ , **April 4, 2009 press conference** –"I believe in American exceptionalism, just as I suspect that the Brits believe in British exceptionalism and the Greeks believe in Greek exceptionalism"

[17] https://fas.org/sgp/crs/row/R40213.pdf

It seems to me that if we do not think of America as an exceptional nation and come right out and say it like we mean it, like we believe it, then how as a nation can we ever achieve exceptional things? For if we do not believe we are an exceptional nation, how can we be an exceptional people? And if we are not an exceptional people, then we must be an unexceptional people. If a President of this exceptional nation thinks of America and her people, as unexceptional, then he truly must believe that we as a people should be ruled over by those whom he thinks are exceptional, like himself and others in his Party who either think like him or provide much for him. And these problems multiply as those in the other Parties think and act in exactly the same way. I think this is one of the greatest problems of modern America today. We have let the Parties and the leaders of those Parties think and talk for us. We have even gone so far as to let the Political Parties and their support groups design the way people of this great Republic may speak to one another. And if someone does not speak in that precisely defined way or act in their prescribed way of acting, then that someone, or that group of someone's is ridiculed. They are called radicals, homophobes, Zionists, racists, or a thousand other ugly words designed to do one thing and only one thing -- shut up the American people. We have come to call this form of speech "politically correct" which is just another way of silencing the good people of America and giving voice to the Parties and the political-media. It must stop if we are to keep this nation an exceptional nation and her people as an exceptional people. We must end the times of power and privilege for only those in political power, their wealthy supporters in business, in Hollywood, and those in the media who feed on their leftovers, their lies, and their political scraps.

I know that the basic and most important thing this nation was founded upon was *to protect the individual rights of the people*, the citizens of this

---

¹⁸ http://yquotes.com/quotes/colin-powell/#ixzz4wmsaBZHg

great Republic, and to make sure that those who infringe upon those individual rights are punished to the full extent of the law no matter who they are, even if one is the wife of an ex-President or an out-of-work Secretary of State. After all, that is what our Constitution was written for, to spell out to our Government what cannot be done to "We the People" and what must be done to those who break the law. This is why we see so much push back from the politicians in both Houses of Congress and several previous Presidencies when it comes to the Constitution, especially since the early 1900's Progressives that Hillary Clinton seems to be so proud of being a part of as she so vehemently announced in her first run for President.[19] I bet if she knew of their racist background…wait a minute, she did know about Senator Bird's racist background… Never mind. What we do see in America today is something the power-privileged have come to call "hate crimes". Now I ask you, are not all violent crimes "hate crimes"? And how is it that one is punished more for the murder of someone of a different color or sex or religion than the murderer of someone of their own type and kind? Put them to death twice? Make them serve two life sentences? As if that could ever hold true in a country where ALL MEN ARE CREATED EQUAL! Does it not make more sense and better sense to punish all who commit any crime to the full extent of the law no matter what? Would it not make perfect sense that someone, anyone, would think twice before committing any crime if that criminal, NO MATTER WHAT COLOR, SEX, OR RELIGION they were, knew that they must, by law, be punished to the full extent of that law without the possibility of their term shortened for good behavior, or early parole? Calling a crime a hate crime is just another way of dividing the American people into camps of color, sex,

---

[19] http://humanevents.com/2007/08/15/what-is-a-progressive/ August 15, 2007, CNN/YouTube debate, "I prefer the word 'progressive,' which has a real American meaning, going back to the progressive era at the beginning of the 20th century. I consider myself a modern progressive."

religion, or whatever the Parties think of next. After all, most Americans today are people of many diverse backgrounds. Check out your DNA, your family tree, and see for yourself if we are not a people of many nations, of many colors. That is what makes us great. We are the world because we are made up of the world. But know that before we are of this color or of this sex or of this religion that we are Americans first, and Americans without the division of the hyphen. For example, I am no more a Danish-English-Scottish-Native American-American than a man of different colors is, you know, a purple-blue-pink-American. There should be NO GREATER CRIME in this great Republic of ours than that of COMMITTING A CRIME AGAINST ANOTHER AMERICAN.

***

Let us move on now to immigration. Some on the Left and on the Right today would have us believe that we are a nation of immigrants, which we are, but how did that happen? Did we simply open up our boarders and let everyone in who wanted in, like some would have us believe? Like is happening today? No. There were rules. If you were sick, you could not enter. If you were a polygamist or if you had no money, you could not enter. If you had no skills or visible means of supporting yourself, you could not enter. You see, way back then in the late 1800's and early 1900's at the height of American immigration, the Government was worried about folks coming to this country and overwhelming the existing American wage earners by being willing to work for even lower wages than they were. They also worried about immigrants compromising our wellbeing by bringing disease to the country or by being a drag on the economy because they had no work skills or that they were criminals. You see, way back then in the time of common sense when people were people and not pawns of the Political Parties, there was no welfare system to save us from ourselves, from our laziness, like there is today.

What we must remember in today's America is that the lowest wage earners are the workers who have little education and work for the lowest wages paid in this country. These are America's poorest, you know, poor white Americans, poor black Americans, and poor brown Americans. They are the very Americans who today are being pushed into even deeper poverty by those who are crossing our southern border by the millions and are willing to work under the table for five dollars an hour or less, you know, the kind of workers who the United States Chamber of Commerce just loves to work to death. When the U.S. Chamber of Commerce promotes an illegal immigrant workforce that is willing to work for less than a living wage for its member companies, they are promoting nothing less than modern slavery.[20]

Add to this exploitation the tons of illicit drugs crossing our southern border that feed this nation's drug epidemic…But, hey, if it will get one Political Party or another more votes and more power, then down with the wall.

The following is from the United States Citizenship and Immigration Service:

"The federal government assumed direct control of inspecting, admitting, rejecting, and processing all immigrants seeking admission to the United States with the Immigration Act of 1891." The 1891 Act also expanded the list of excludable classes, barring the immigration of polygamists, persons convicted of crimes of moral turpitude, and those suffering loathsome or contagious diseases.

---

[20] http://www.bing.com/search?q=u+s+chamber+of+commerce+on+immigration&form=U164DF&pc=U164

The national government's new immigration obligations and its increasingly complex immigration laws required a dedicated federal enforcement agency to regulate immigration. Accordingly, the 1891 Immigration Act created the Office of the Superintendent of Immigration within the Treasury Department. The Superintendent oversaw a new corps of U.S. Immigrant Inspectors stationed at the country's principal ports of entry.

Federal Immigration Stations

On January 2, 1892, the Immigration Service opened the U.S.'s best known immigration station on Ellis Island in New York Harbor. The enormous station housed inspection facilities, hearing and detention rooms, hospitals, cafeterias, administrative offices, railroad ticket offices, and representatives of many immigrant aid societies. America's largest and busiest port of entry for decades, Ellis Island station employed 119 of the Immigration Service's entire staff of 180 in 1893.

The Service built additional immigrant stations at other principal ports of entry through the early 20th century. At New York, Boston, Philadelphia, and other traditional ports of entry, the Immigration Service hired many Immigrant Inspectors who previously worked for state agencies. At other ports, both old and new, the Service built an Inspector corps by hiring former Customs Inspectors and Chinese Inspectors, and training recruits.

Implementing A National Immigration Policy

During its first decade, the Immigration Service formalized basic immigration procedures and made its first attempts to enforce a national immigration policy. The Immigration Service began   collecting arrival manifests (also frequently called passenger lists or immigration arrival records) from each incoming ship, a former duty of the U.S. Customs Service since 1820. Inspectors then questioned arrivals about their admissibility and noted their admission or rejection on the manifest records.

Beginning in 1893, Inspectors also served on Boards of Special Inquiry that closely reviewed each exclusion case. Inspectors often initially excluded aliens who were likely to become public charges because they lacked funds or had no friends or relatives nearby. In these cases, the Board of Special Inquiry usually admitted the alien if someone could post bond or one of the immigrant aid societies would accept responsibility for the alien.

Detention guards and matrons cared for detained persons pending decisions in their cases or, if the decision was negative, awaiting deportation. The Immigration Service deported aliens denied admission by the Board of Special Inquiry at the expense of the transportation company that brought them to the port.

Enhanced Responsibilities

Congress continued to exert Federal control over immigration with the Act of March 2, 1895, which promoted the Office of Immigration to the Bureau of Immigration and changed the agency head's title from Superintendent to Commissioner-General of Immigration. The Act of June 6, 1900, consolidated immigration enforcement by assigning enforcement of both Alien Contract Labor laws and Chinese Exclusion laws to the Commissioner-General.

Because most immigration laws of the time sought to protect American workers and wages, an Act of February 14, 1903, transferred the Bureau of Immigration from the Treasury Department to the newly created

Department of Commerce and Labor. An "immigrant fund" created from collection of immigrants' head tax financed the Immigration Service until 1909, when Congress replaced the fund with an annual appropriation."[21]

So why is it that there are so many today who want open borders? It's simple. Those in the know have come to the conclusion that those who cross into this country illegally are far more likely to vote Democrat than Republican. So you can see that even this is just another Party power-play to give one Party more power than the other and has absolutely nothing to do with making America a better country nor to bettering the lives of all Americans and immigrants, but instead is designed to make America a Leftist controlled country in which the poorest citizens are forced to work for less and less with no hope for upward mobility. In other words, those empowered by the Democrat Party and their Hollywood cronies say to open the borders as long as the immigrants and poor citizens can never live in their Malibu neighborhoods or in certain wealthy counties around Washington, D.C. unless they happen to be live-in maids, servants, or chauffeurs. And Republican Party members want the borders left open for the benefit of the U. S. Chamber of Commerce which wants immigrants from Mexico who are willing to work for less than a living wage therefore bolstering the profits of large Republican companies that donate to the Republican Party, for these are the companies that give immense donations to Republican Party candidates. That's why there has been little done to stop the illegal crossings for at least three generations.

***

Frederick Douglass was a slave who, after he was freed, became one of this country's leading abolitionist writers and speakers. He was the

---

[21] https://www.uscis.gov/history-and-genealogy/our-history/agency-history/origins-federal-immigration-service

most photographed American in the 19th century. One of the topics he spoke on was "Popular Error and Unpopular Truth." In this speech Douglas said; "There [is] no such thing as new truth. Error might be old or new; but truth is as old as the universe." He believed in this country and in this country's founding documents. He believed that words contained in these documents, words like "all men are created equal"; that they are "endowed by their Creator [and certainly not by any earthly government] with certain unalienable Rights" among which are "Life, Liberty, and the pursuit of Happiness" and that "to secure these rights governments are instituted among men." Mr. Douglas called these "the saving principles" and he became devoted to convincing all Americans to trust in these principles.[22]

I wish that all of the people we see fighting in our streets today knew these things, knew that it was not government that gave the people these things, but God, even as we can feel deep within us that these things, these words are true and real and they are born deep within every human soul regardless of color or sex. We all want to be free when it comes right down to it, so why is it that we are fighting in the streets to have our government bind us down with chains again? We simply must remember that Frederick Douglass was no racist, and he even called race pride "a positive evil " and a "false foundation " on which to base anything that might be expected to last and thrive.[23]

****

We must learn from our mistakes. Historically, anything that Government gives to the people or to any community has something

---

[22] Imprimis, Hillsdale College, Frederick Douglass, American, July/August 2017, Volume 46, Number 7/8, Lucas E. Morel https://imprimis.hillsdale.edu/frederick-douglass-american/

[23] Ibid.

nefarious that those Government givers are reaching for, like votes or monetary payoff or the silencing of their adversary, and the outcome never really benefits the citizens as much as it does the Parties.

Examples:

• Paying the unwed mother for each child born without a sir name has brought about the ruin of the family, especially Black families, by the removal of the father, or at least the need of a father, from the home.[24]

• Eliminating the unborn by the millions, mostly from black families, just as Margaret Sanger dreamed of, while sugar coating it as "pro-choice."[25]

• Creating housing loans for people who obviously will never be able to repay them, then through Party line legislation and signed by Pres. Bill Clinton himself, forcing the banks to forgive these loans, thus giving free housing to probable voters in the next election while simultaneously bringing about the ruin of small banks and loan companies whose members would presumably vote for a different Party.[26]

This is the hallmark of identity politics, of political division. This is the hallmark of a biased media defending what their chosen Party does or does not do. And this is the hallmark of countrymen turning against countrymen simply to give one Party or another more power, more fame, and yes, more riches.

I do not know about you, but I know how I feel, or how I have been made to feel by a government that always seems stuck in some political mire or another, never getting anything done for the people, *their employers*, but only for their Party's benefit. Over and over again we listen to

---

[24] *Liberalism or How to Turn Good Men into Whiners, Weenies and Wimps, Burgess Owens*, (copyright 2016, Post Hill Press, first edition)

[25] http://www.blackgenocide.org/sanger.html

[26] http://www.bizpacreview.com/2011/10/24/jimmy-carter-bill-clinton-janet-reno-to-blame-for-mortgage-mess-704

some pale excuse by some loud mouth Senator or another who has been a Senator since most of us were just kids and is never seen in anything less than a ten thousand dollar suit matched with two thousand dollar shoes. It makes one wonder just how it is that a person who works for you and me and was once financially equal to most of his constituents, can get so extremely wealthy on a Senator's or a Congressman's salary. It almost makes "my eyes shoot blood, and my head explode" to quote the popular radio show host Glenn Beck. I have finally come to that boiling point of believing that the only thing the Republican Party or the Democrat Party really cares about these days, especially on the Federal level, is the Party and the power and privilege the Party brings to its elected members. I truly believe that the Parties and their politicians couldn't care less about the American people who voted them into office, the people who put campaign signs in their yards, made phone calls on their behalf, went to debates just to cheer on their Party man or woman, donated their own hard earned money to a Party they think will support them in their needs. I have come to the conclusion that the only time the Parties care about the people is just before Election Day. The rest of the two to six years between elections the only thing they care about is the Party -- not the people but the Party -- and the good things the Party can hand out to them. They cannot remember your name and they really wish you would just go away quietly without a hand shake and stop bothering them so that they can enjoy the spoils of their victory in the swamp with the rest of the wealthy alligators.

****

Yes, the only time the Political Parties care about the people of this once great nation of ours is at election time, and yes, it behooves them to keep us at each other's throats the rest of the time. It behooves the Political Parties, in this polarized political climate, to keep the American people divided one against the other. It behooves the Political Parties to stir up hatreds between family members, friends, neighbors, brothers, and sisters. It behooves the Political Parties to stir up anger and hatred in the hearts of Americans with lies and innuendoes, because angry Americans *vote*, and your vote is the only thing a true Party man or woman really cherishes.

This is why in my opinion it's time for Political Parties to come to a quick and painless end, like the pulling of a Band-Aid from a very hairy arm. I, for one, applaud the notion, and I hope you do too. We must, for the love of our country, for the love of our family, and for the love of God, bring a speedy END TO THE POLITICAL PARTIES before the Parties bring an end to the Divinely inspired America we love, live in, cherish, and respect.

Some would argue that we need a new Third Party, but it, too, would sooner than later devolve into just another power hungry, selfish, egoistic Political Party.

How do we end the Party System? We can begin by stopping the flow of money and votes to them. **STOP DONATING TO THE POLITICAL PARTIES. STOP VOTING FOR PARTY MEN AND WOMEN.**

Party Politicians use money to fund smear campaigns, to advertise embellished lies about themselves, and to promote themselves to businesses and other big money sources thereby committing themselves to return favors to their big donors and not to keeping their promises to us little guys, the voting public, the people they are supposed to be serving. Then when they get elected, reelected, re-reelected, they throw lavish celebrations, inviting only the big money donors, not the average voter/donor. Facebook CEO Mark Zuckerberg's vote should be no more important than that of John Smith, kindergarten teacher.

Even with big money donors, without smaller donations from millions of folks, regular citizens, like you and me, the Parties would go hungry for funds. People who want to donate money to help someone get elected should give to the individual they think will do a good and honorable job in office, preferably someone who does not have a Party listed before his or her name. Forget the Party donations. These only pay to bring more and more injustice to our political system.

***

Why does any of this matter? you might ask. It matters because everyone should know that in a country that is run by the Government, especially of either Left or Right extreme, the only ones who prosper are those in the Government and their families and friends. That is why today half of the ten wealthiest counties in the United States are those counties that surround Washington, D.C.[27]   It reminds me of the hierarchy of Monarchs of old with their kingdoms and surrounding provinces run by Dukes, Duchesses, Earls, and other royal family members and their friends, while all the *common people's* money ran like a river into the rulers' pockets. Those unwilling to give were soon housed in the local chamber of horrors.

Unfortunately, the Political Parties and their self-serving Politicians, in conjunction with their lapdogs in the Media, have an all too powerful force in American Politics. These Parties have progressed to a point of power in the last few decades where they have conveniently forgotten the goals and promises they made to the American people. They have buried the American people -- our generation, our children and grandchildren -- under a staggering amount of debt and pushed the Constitution aside, all in order to enrich themselves and their own families and friends and donors. **THIS MUST END!**

We the People must study and preserve our history and the

---

[27] https://www.forbes.com/sites/rebeccalerner/2017/07/13/top-10-richest-counties-in-america-2017/#34558a3b2ef3

Constitution, including the Bill of Rights, which protect our Liberties. There are many factors and factions that make this seem like an impossible goal, but we Americans have always succeeded when doing the impossible. A good starting point is to put the Parties in their place by ***defunding*** them and refusing to vote for their candidates. These Parties have divided the People of America for far too long for their own Political gains. It is high time we end this mockery and become **ONE AMERICA**.

In a country that is *run by the people*, every individual has an equal opportunity to prosper.

✱✱✱

"When misguided public opinion honors what is despicable and despises what is honorable, punishes virtue and rewards vice, encourages what is harmful and discourages what is useful, applauds falsehood and smothers truth under indifference or insult, a nation turns its back on progress and can be restored only by the terrible lessons of catastrophe."— *Frederic Bastiat*

✱✱✱

In conclusion, I call upon the wisdom of Frederic Bastiat and paraphrase one of his many thoughts on politics. Must we wait until we have learned by experience, even cruel experience, to trust in the institutions of the state a little less and in each other a little more.[28]

For this I pray.

---

[28] *The Law*, Frederic Bastiat (copyright 2007, Foundation for Economic Freedom, November 2010 edition) p. 62.

Suggested Reading

1.   *George Washington's Sacred Fire*, Peter A. Lillback, (copyright 2006, Dickinson Press, first edition)

2.   *Liberalism or How to Turn Good Men into Whiners, Weenies and Wimps*, Burgess Owens, (copyright 2016, Post Hill Press, first edition)

3.   *The Federalist Papers: A Collection of Essays Written in Favour of the New Constitution*, Alexander Hamilton, James Madison, John Jay, (copyright 2015, Coventry House Publishing)

4.   *The 5000 Year Leap*, W. Cleon Skousen, (copyright 1981, National Center for Constitutional Studies, April 2009 edition)

5.   *The Law*, Frederic Bastiat (copyright 2007, Foundation for Economic Freedom, November 2010 edition)

6.   *The Real Benjamin Franklin: The True Story of America's Greatest Diplomat, (American Classic Series)*, Andrew M. Allison, (copyright 1982, 2008, National Center for Constitutional Studies)

7.   *The Real George Washington: The True Story of America's Most Indispensable Man (American Classic Series)*, Jay A. Parry, Andrew M. Allison, W. Cleon Skousen, (copyright 1991, 2008, National Center for Constitutional Studies)

8.   *The Real Thomas Jefferson: The True Story of America's Philosopher of Freedom (American Classic Series), Andrew M. Allison, (copyright 1983, 2008, National Center for Constitutional Studies)*

Also visit

- National Center for Constitutional Studies https://nccs.net/
- Providence Forum - Reviving the Spirit of Liberty www.providenceforum.org
- https://imprimis.hillsdale.edu/ free monthly speech digest of Hillsdale College dedicated to educating citizens and promoting civil and religious liberty

ABOUT THE AUTHOR

uTAH jAY© is a former U.S. Marine, campaign manager, and three-time county delegate for the State of Utah. He is an artist, sculptor, and photographer who would like to see the citizens of our United States of America work together to return our Federal Government to the People.

***

"Let it simply be asked, where is the security for property, for reputation, for life, if the sense of religious obligation desert the oaths which are the instruments of investigation in our courts of justice?" -- George Washington

***

"The religious man puts his soul on the line in today's courts, so let the non-believer put his wealth on the line, that in our courts of justice, truth may at last be found." -- uTAH jAY©